PERPETUUM JAZZiLE

Vocal Ecstasy

POP SERIES

Volume 1

ISBN 978-1-5400-0043-9

7777 W. BLUEMOUND RD. P.O. BOX 13819 MILWAUKEE, WI 53213

Visit Hal Leonard Online at
www.halleonard.com

Need help?

http://www.perpetuumjazzile.si/workshops

AFRICA

Words and Music by DAVID PAICH and JEFF PORCARO
Arranged by TOMAŽ KOZLEVČAR

www.perpetuumjazzile.si/workshops

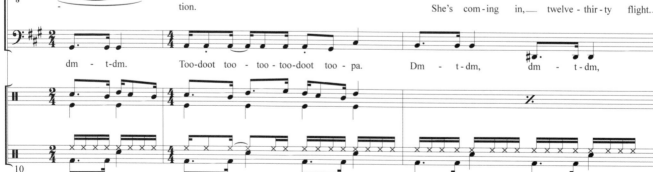

EARTH WIND & FIRE MEDLEY

In The Stone, September and *Boogie Wonderland*

Arranged by TOMAŽ KOZLEVČAR

VOCAL ECSTASY

20

you home, yeah, yea - ee, ar, writ - ten in the stone.
k - dn tn tn tn tn tn k - dn tn tn tn tn tn k - dn tn tn tn tn tn
aw aw pap
Love,
writ - ten in the stone.
aw aw pap
te - ge de - ge tem te - ge de - ge tem te - ge de - ge tem tem
38
41
Do you be - lieve, my friend, in what you claim?
Peo - ple of the world all doubt
k - dn tn tn tn tn tn k - dn tn tn tn tn tn k - dn tn tn tn tn tn
ta - ga - da
ta - ga - da
tem tem tem tem tem te - ke - de tem tem tem
41

22

September

Boogie Wonderland
Words and Music by John Lind and Allee Willis

30

Mid-night creeps so— slow - ly in - to— hearts of men who need more than they get.

ee

tm - de - dm tm - dm tm - tm tm tm - dm— tm - de - dm tm - de - dm tm tm tm tm - dm

32

The mir - ror stares____ you in____ the face____ and says,____ "Ba - by, uh,____ uh,____ it____ don't work."

twee - dap   pap

pa - dap   pap

pa - dap

tm - de - dm   tm - dm   tm - tm   tm   tm - dm____ tm - de - dm   tm - de - dm   tm   tm   tm   tm - dm____

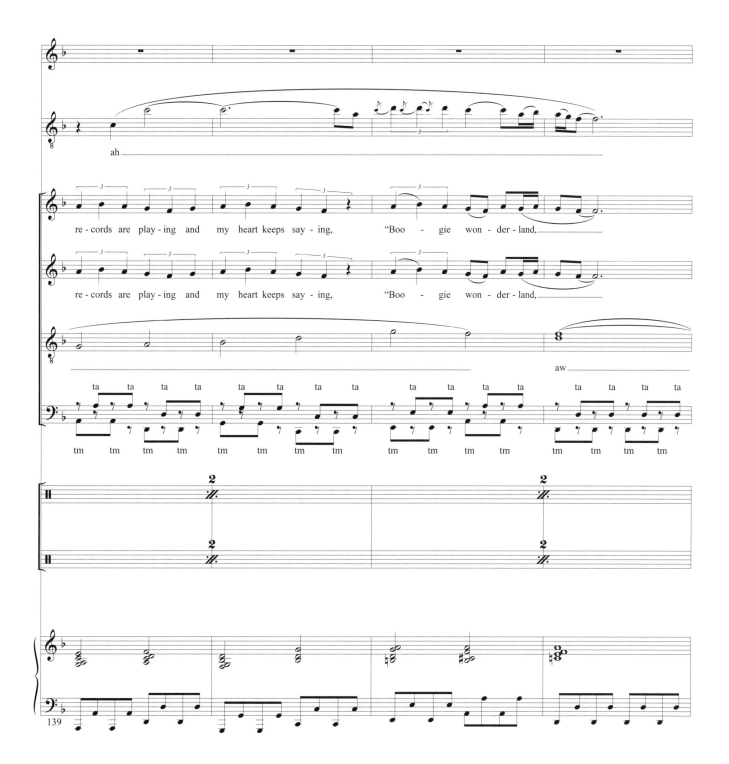

land.___ Ha, ha, dance, boo - gie won - der -

oo oo oo oo dance___ yeah___

pa-dap pa-dap

pap pap Ha, ha, pa-dap pa-dap

pap pap Ha, ha, pa-dap-pa-dap te-ge de-ge-de-ge de-ge-de-ge

___ tm-de - dm tm-de-dm tm tm tm tm - dm tm - de - dm tm - dm tm - tm tm tm - dm___

148

164

JOYFUL, JOYFUL

Words by HENRY VAN DYKE
Additional rap lyrics by RYAN TOBY

Music arranged by MERVIN WARREN
Based on Ludwig van Beethoven's *Symphony No. 9*
Adapted by TOMAŽ KOZLEVČAR

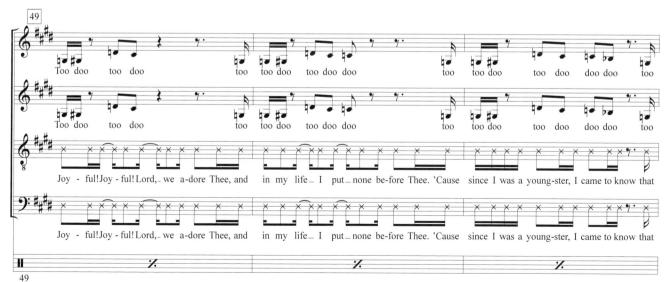

48

VOCAL ECSTASY

What Have You Done For Me Lately

What Have You Done For Me Lately

JUST THE WAY YOU ARE

Words and Music by BILLY JOEL
Arranged by TOMAŽ KOVLEVČAR

58

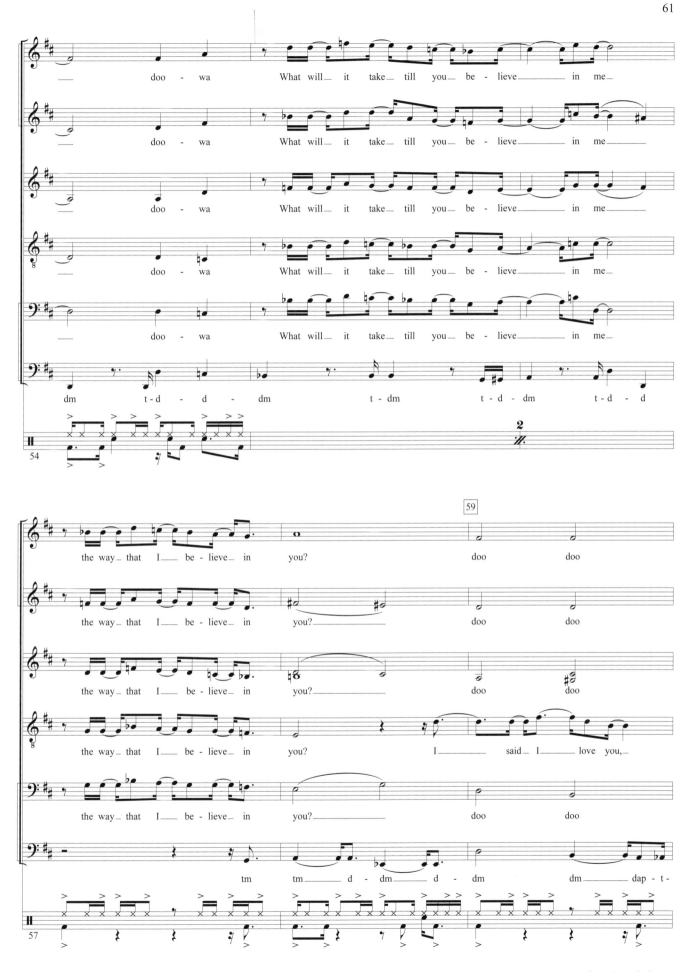

VOCAL ECSTASY

VOCAL ECSTASY

OH HAPPY DAY

Words and Music by EDWIN R. HAWKINS
Arranged by TOMAŽ KOZLEVČAR

www.perpetuumjazzile.si/workshops

68

VOCAL ECSTASY

Oo hoo. Oo hoo. Oo hoo.

Oo hoo. Oo hoo. Oo hoo.

Oo hoo. Oo hoo. Oo hoo.

Oo hoo. Oo hoo. Oo hoo.

Oo hoo. Oo hoo. Oo hoo.

Oo hoo, oo hoo.

Oo hoo, oo hoo.

Oo hoo, oo hoo.

Oo hoo, oo hoo.

Oo hoo, oo hoo.

ROSANNA

Words and Music by DAVID PAICH
Arranged by TOMAŽ KOZLEVČAR

To Coda ⊕

VOCAL ECSTASY

san - na, Ro - san - na.

I nev-er thought that los-in' you__ could ev-er hurt so__ bad.__

p

oo__

tad-dle tad-dle tad-dle__ tad-dle tad-dle oo

tad-dle tad-dle tad-dle__ tad-dle__

ff

san - na, Ro - san - na.__ da

da

dk k-ta__ k-dk k-ta k-ta-ga k-tm__ -dm__ tm -dm tm tm tm -dm__ tm -dm tm tm

44

Male Quartet

tad - dle tad - dle tad-dle tad-dle - tem

tem - dem tem - dem tem

fp *ff*

na, yeah. da

fp *ff*

na, yeah. da

fp

na, yeah. tad-dle-de de-dl-de tel-de-de de-dl-de tad-dle-de

fp

na, yeah.

ten-den ten-den__ dk k-ta k-dk k-ta k-ta-ga k-

47

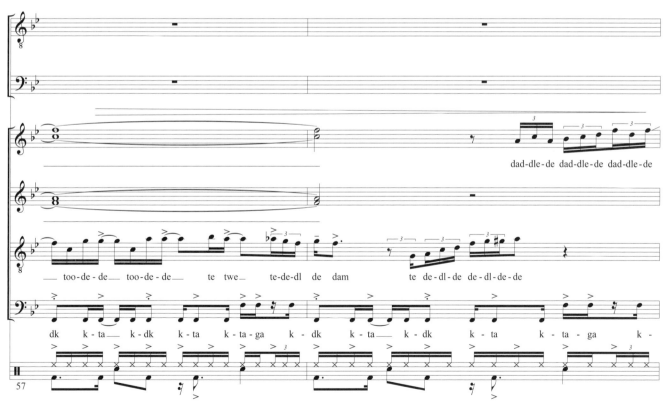

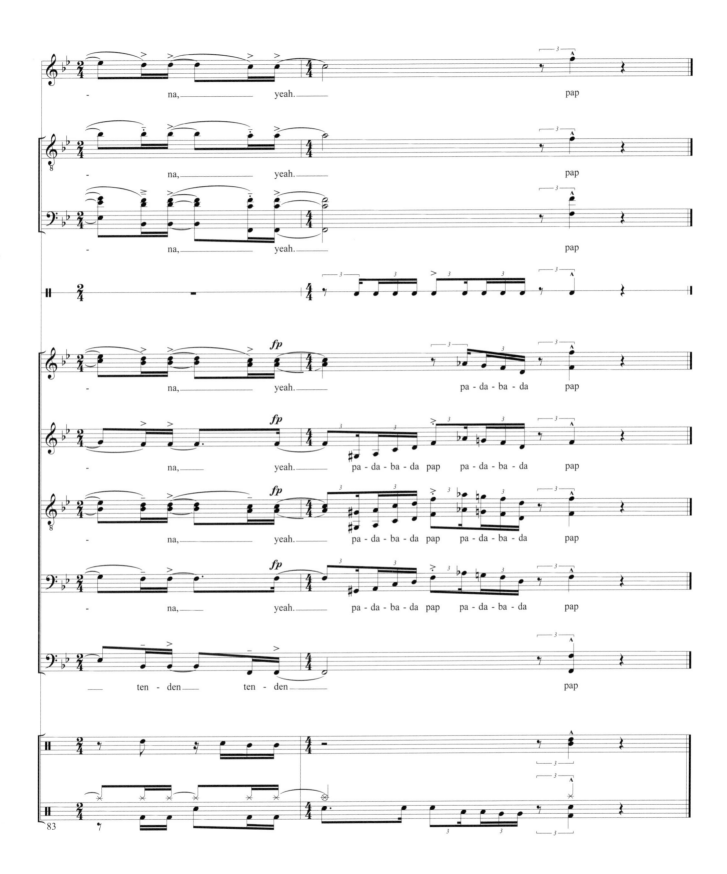

TRUE COLORS

Words and Music by BILLY STEINBERG and TOM KELLY
Arranged by TOMAŽ KOZLEVČAR

VOCAL ECSTASY

100

VOCAL ECSTASY

95

too - doo too - doo too - doo - doo

- ors shine. So beau-ti-ful. That's why I love you.

Show me your rain - bow. Show me your col-

Show me your rain - bow. That's why I love you. Show me your col-

Show me your rain - bow. Show me your col-

tum - duk tum tum - duk tum - duk tum tum - duk tum

101